Computer Programming for Kids
with Scratch 2.0

3rd Edition

Craig Whitmore

Published by Craig Whitmore
Bakersfield, CA

ISBN 978-1-312-29659-6

© 2011-14, Craig Whitmore

Third Edition

Disclaimer

This is a book by an educator intended for use by other educators. It is designed to be handed out to a class of 30+ middle school boys and girls (some of whom may not really want to be there) in a 45 minute-long introductory elective class. The design of this book allows teachers to engage the wide variety of students one finds in a middle school class. Most students will not take the time to read printed instructions (really, who does these days?), but can and will follow visual examples. This book makes use of that observation.

While I have used these tutorials day-in and day-out for seven years (with over 1,000 5th-8th grade students), I don't simply hand them out and expect the students to do it on their own. I would suggest that the teacher study these tutorials beforehand and even make them along with the students on a display device.

Additionally, these tutorials are meant as starting points – I generally require my students to make two or three changes to each program for full credit. Without doubt your students will discover new and interesting things to do with Scratch that you did not envision. Encourage and praise them when they do this. Such self-expression is what programming is really all about.

Dedications

First, to my Lord and Savior, Jesus Christ:
You are my reason for living. Any good I do comes from You.
"From You and through You and to You are all things.
To You be glory forever! Amen!" (Romans 11:36)

Second, to my wife of 16 years, Tara: "Thanks" doesn't quite cover all that
you mean to me. I love being your husband!

Finally, to my kids, Kayleigh, Tyler, Zachary, Jarren, and Becca: Being your father
is one of the greatest blessings God has given to me! Remember life is good,
eternal life is better!

Table of Contents

Introduction to Scratch
What is Scratch?
What has Changed between 1.4 and 2.0?
The Scratch 2 Environment
Scratch 2 Intro Worksheet

Tutorial Programs
Beginning Level
1. Using the Paint Editor
2. Creating Backgrounds
3. Create-a-Scene
4. Changing Graphic Effects – Crazy Cat
5. Controlling Movement – Three Methods
6. Changing Costumes – Celebrity DressUp
7. Changing Costumes - Autobiography Collage
8. Using Instruments - Making Music
9. Drawing Commands – Name Art
10. Using Hide and Show – Hidden Objects

Intermediate Level
11. Using Conditionals – Maze
12. Game #1 – Platforms
13. Simulating Gravity – Jumping Cat
14. Asking Questions – Quiz Show
15. Game #2 – Pong
16. Using a "Missile" – Hit the Target
17. Intermediate Art – Recreate a Landscape
18. Game #3 – Asteroids
19. Using Animated Gifs – Target Shooting
20. Using Layers – Sniper Game

Advanced Level
21. Using Instruments – Create-a-Song
22. Game #4 – Pac-Man
23. Using Scrolling Backgrounds – Cat Walk
24. Simulating 3D – Come Closer
25. Using the Pen Commands – Etch-a-Sketch Art
26. Using Lists – Number Guessing Game
27. Create Your Own Retro Game
28. Create Your Own Original Game
29. Real World Challenge #1 – Office Security Lighting
30. Real World Challenge #2 – Debugging Bug Bounce

Additional Worksheets
Reflection Sheets for Programs
Retro Game Planning Page
Retro Game Review Page
Original Game Planning Page
Original Game Report
Scratch Online Program Review
Scratch Commands Crossword

Appendices
A – The Coordinate System in Scratch
B – Using the Paint Editor
C – Music Basics
D – Programming Code Help Sheet
E – Going Further with Scratch-style Programming (Code.org and Snap!)

What is Scratch?

Scratch is a computer programming language written by the Lifelong Kindergarten group at the MIT Media Lab. It was introduced in 2007 with the goal of introducing students to programming languages. Scratch allows users to program by simply clicking programming code blocks together. It is a dynamic, object-oriented, event-driven language. The current version is 2.0.

Scratch is free to download. It is also OS agnostic, meaning it works and (more importantly) looks the same on Windows, MacOS, and Linux. It comes complete with over 650 sprite images, more than 70 backgrounds, over 80 sound effects and nearly 80 example programs.

The Scratch website is http://scratch.mit.edu. There is a Scratch online community where programmers can share, comment, tag, download and remix programs they write and upload to the site. There are over 600,000 registered members and over 5,400,000 projects have been shared online. You do not have to register to download Scratch, use Scratch, or view the programs others have uploaded online.

A creative learning community with **5,473,252** projects shared

Programming Blocks

Scratch uses programming blocks (sometimes called bricks or tiles) to control what happens in the program. Each block has underlying computer code that tells the program what to do in a language it understands (Java). Each block has been grouped with like blocks and painted the same color. For example, all the motion blocks are a dark blue. Each set of blocks can be found in their own "drawer", located in the upper center of the program. Usually, the blocks control individual "sprites".

Sprites

A sprite is a graphic element that can be moved as one piece. Sprites can be turned, shrunk, have their color altered, and collisions between sprites can be detected. The default sprite when you open Scratch is the cat, which has two costumes and one sound preloaded. There are several ways to get or modify sprites in Scratch, including drawing your own, importing one of Scratch's, and importing images stored on your computer (making it eay to use almost any online image you find and save).

What has changed between 1.4 and 2.0?

- Backgrounds now called "backdrops" (**Stage**)
- Addded **Tips** to lead you through each type of block and various programming styles
- Added ability to create your own blocks (**More Blocks**)
- The **Image Editor** can now convert from vector to bitmap art (Scratch 1.4 was always bitmapped).
- Revamped the **instruments** and **percussion**. There are now less choices, but all of them seem to work (not the case in Scratch 1.4)

Code block additions

- "Set Rotation Style" block so rotation can be changed within a script (**Motion**)
- "when backdrop switches to …" block (**Events**)
- "when (loudness) > …" block (**Events**)
- "switch backdrop to …" – allows sprite to control backdrop of stage (**Looks**)
- cloning code blocks (**Control**)
- video motion blocks (**Sensing**)
- ability to show / hide variable value within a script (**Data**)

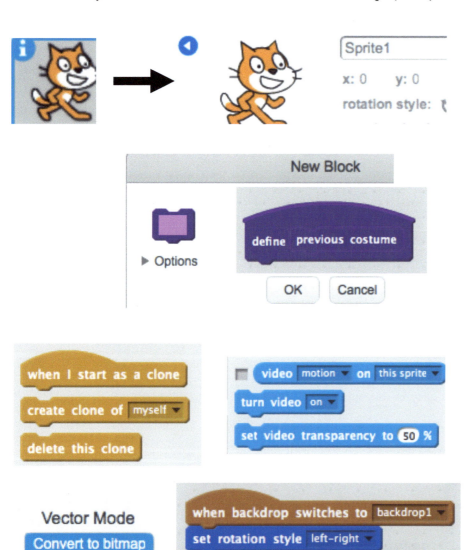

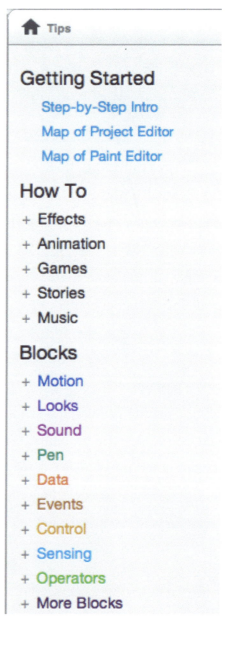

The Scratch 2 Environment

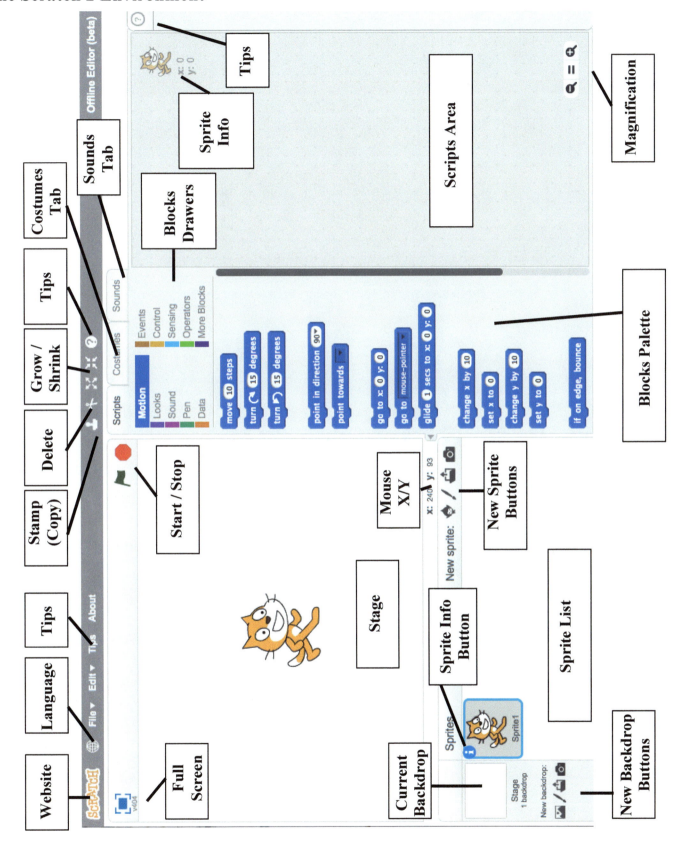

The Scratch 2 Environment

NAME _____

PER _____ DATE _____

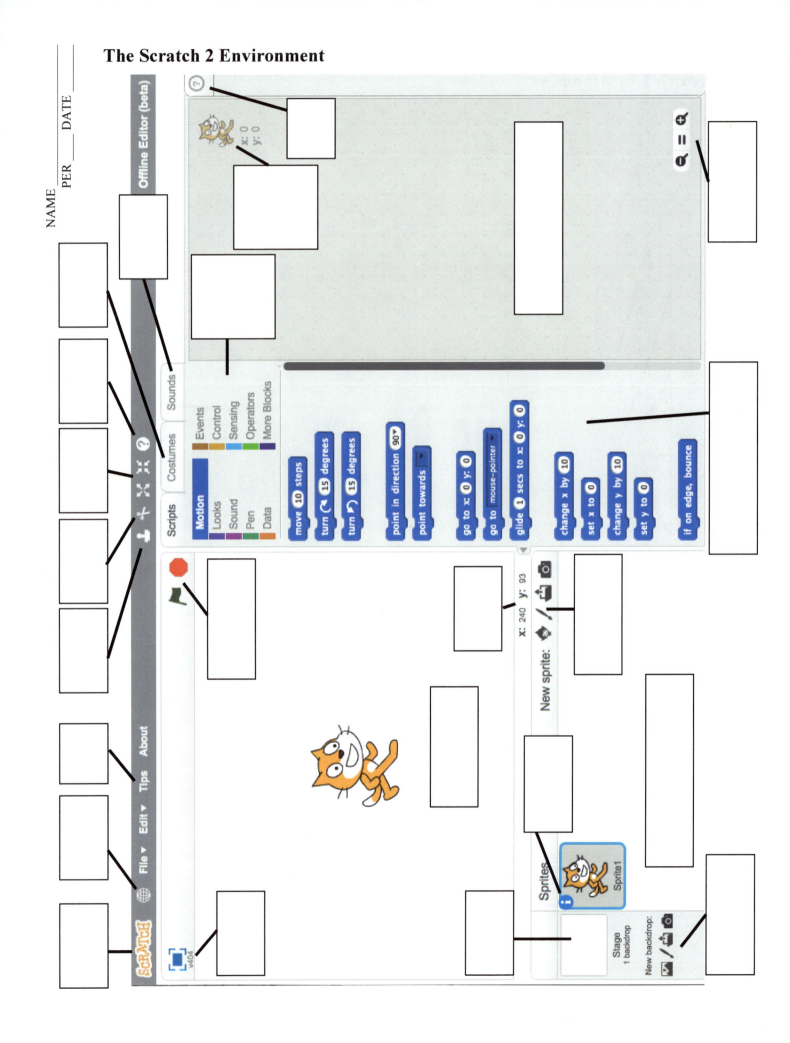

Scratch 2 Intro Worksheet

1. What are the 10 "blocks drawers" in the upper middle?

2. What is the top brick called in the (**Sound**) drawer?

3. Which drawer has a brick labeled (**ask<what's your name?> and wait**)?

4. What else might you call the (**Operators**) drawer?

5. How many bricks are in the (**Looks**) drawer?

6. What is the default setting for the (**set pen size to #**) brick?

7. What is the last brick in the (**Control**) drawer?

8. How many graphic effects can you choose between for the (**change <color> effect by <25>**) brick in the (**Looks**) drawer?

9. What color is the (**Sensing**) drawer?

10. What color is the (**Pen**) drawer?

11. What is the **white globe** for (upper left)?

12. What happens if you click on the name "**Scratch**" in the upper left corner?

13. What is the real name of the stamp tool in the upper bar?

14. What does clicking on the blue rectangle at the upper left do?

15. In the middle of the Scratch screen, what does the **paintbrush button** do?

16. How many theme folders are in the **Sprite Library**?

17. How many **costumes** does the original cat have preloaded?

18. How many **sounds** does the original cat have preloaded?

19. How many choices are in the **Indoors Category** of the **Backdrops Library**?

20. How many options do you have to get a new costume from the top of the "**Costumes**" tab?

Programming Tutorials

1. Using the Paint Editor

1. Click on the "Paint New Sprite" button
2. Create your own person. Use color. Be creative. Have fun.
3. Use the blue Motion drawer and the yellow Control drawer to put together the following code in the Scripts area:

New sprite: **Paint new sprite**

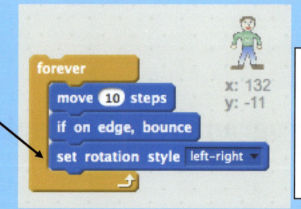

This code block controls the rotation of the sprite. Select "left-right" to stop your person from turning upside-down!

```
forever
    move 10 steps
    if on edge, bounce
    set rotation style left-right ▼
```

x: 132
y: -11

point towards ▼   mouse-pointer

You can also place this block in the forever loop. Click the arrow in the box and select "mouse pointer" to have the sprite chase you around the stage.

4. Make two additions or changes to this program.

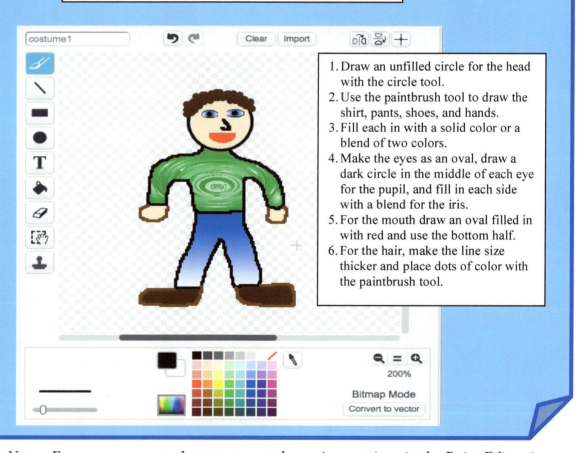

costume1   Clear   Import   200%   Bitmap Mode   Convert to vector

1. Draw an unfilled circle for the head with the circle tool.
2. Use the paintbrush tool to draw the shirt, pants, shoes, and hands.
3. Fill each in with a solid color or a blend of two colors.
4. Make the eyes as an oval, draw a dark circle in the middle of each eye for the pupil, and fill in each side with a blend for the iris.
5. For the mouth draw an oval filled in with red and use the bottom half.
6. For the hair, make the line size thicker and place dots of color with the paintbrush tool.

(Educator's Note: Encourage your students to try out the various settings in the Paint Editor (see Appendix B or the Help Tips within the program). Show them how to experiment with fills and gradients (a great way to make eyes) and how to change the size of the brush and line tools.)

2. Creating Backdrops

1. Click on the "Choose backdrop from library" icon and import one of Scratch's pre-loaded backgrounds.

   Next, click on the "Paint new backdrop" icon.
2. Switch to "Vector Mode" and create a backdrop using filled-in squares and circles.

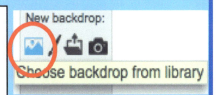

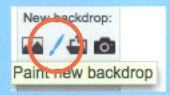

Vector Mode
Convert to bitmap

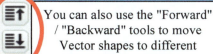

Use the paintcan tool to color in the shapes you make.

You can also use the "Forward" / "Backward" tools to move Vector shapes to different

You can get interesting / artistic looks by using the blend choices at the bottom left. Clicking on the two color squares swaps the foreground and background colors that you are painting with.

Click again on the "Paint new backdrop" icon.
3. This time use the "Bitmap Mode" to create a simple landscape. It helps to <u>start by outlining each area</u>, working from closer to farther away, and then fill them in with horizontal blends.

Bitmap Mode
Convert to vector

3. Importing Sprites – Artistic Scene

- This is an artistic creation, no programming at all, but it will help familiarize you with importing sprites in Scratch.

- Create a scene using at least 10 sprites and/or backgrounds.

- Look around Scratch's preloaded backgrounds and Sprites to get an overall idea in mind.

- Import your background first, then begin adding sprites. The image below contains 4 people, 2 dogs. and 2 items.

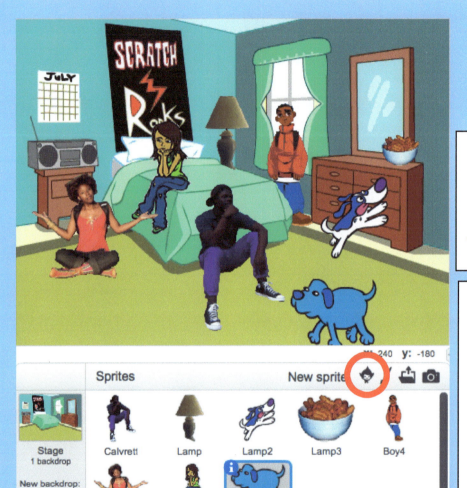

You can use the "grow" and "shrink" buttons to fix the size of your sprites.

You can change a sprite's direction by clicking on and rotating the circle above the selection box.

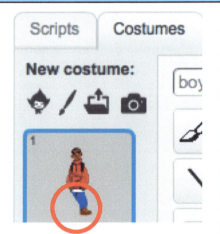

If necessary, you can even edit a sprite (to erase a corner, for instance) by clicking on the "Costumes" tab.

4. Graphic Effects – Crazy Cat

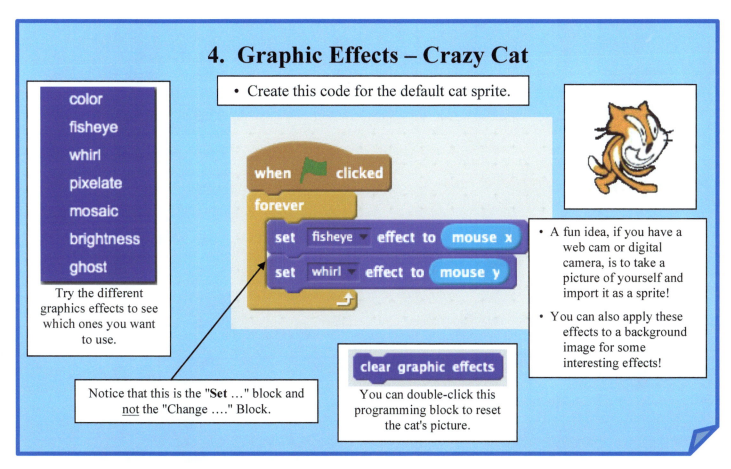

- Create this code for the default cat sprite.

color
fisheye
whirl
pixelate
mosaic
brightness
ghost

Try the different graphics effects to see which ones you want to use.

```
when [green flag] clicked
forever
    set fisheye effect to (mouse x)
    set whirl effect to (mouse y)
```

- A fun idea, if you have a web cam or digital camera, is to take a picture of yourself and import it as a sprite!

- You can also apply these effects to a background image for some interesting effects!

Notice that this is the "**Set …**" block and <u>not</u> the "Change …." Block.

clear graphic effects

You can double-click this programming block to reset the cat's picture.

Scratch uses a Cartesian coordinate system where 0,0 is at the center of the Stage. X and Y increase to the right and up (respectively) and decrease to the left and down (respectively). The Stage measures 480 pixels horizontally (-240 to 240) and 360 pixels vertically (-180 to 180).

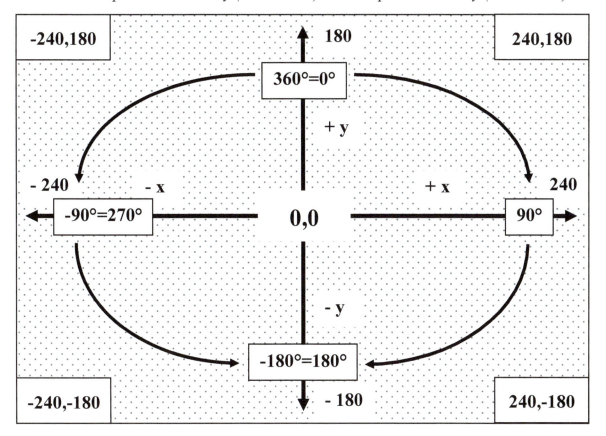

-240,180 | 180 | 240,180

360°=0°

+ y

- 240 | - x | + x | 240

-90°=270° | 0,0 | 90°

- y

-180°=180°

-240,-180 | - 180 | 240,-180

5. Controlling Movement – Three Variations

1. Import three sprites (your choice).

2. Create each of these movement programs for a different one, so you don't get any overlapping code on a single sprite!

3. The usual convention is to use the W-A-S-D keys to control movement for a second player.

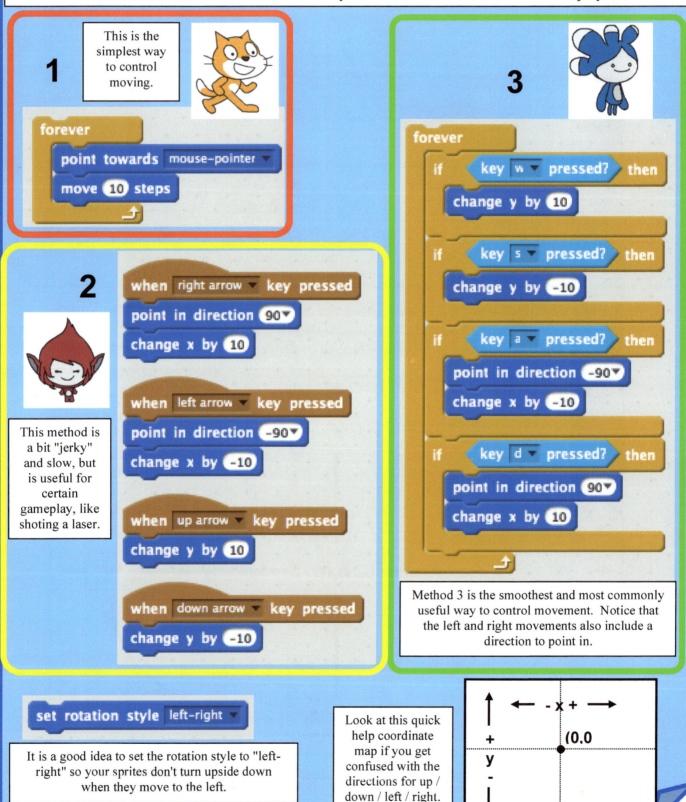

1

This is the simplest way to control moving.

```
forever
    point towards mouse-pointer ▼
    move 10 steps
```

2

This method is a bit "jerky" and slow, but is useful for certain gameplay, like shoting a laser.

```
when right arrow ▼ key pressed
point in direction 90 ▼
change x by 10

when left arrow ▼ key pressed
point in direction -90 ▼
change x by -10

when up arrow ▼ key pressed
change y by 10

when down arrow ▼ key pressed
change y by -10
```

3

```
forever
    if  key w ▼ pressed?  then
        change y by 10

    if  key s ▼ pressed?  then
        change y by -10

    if  key a ▼ pressed?  then
        point in direction -90 ▼
        change x by -10

    if  key d ▼ pressed?  then
        point in direction 90 ▼
        change x by 10
```

Method 3 is the smoothest and most commonly useful way to control movement. Notice that the left and right movements also include a direction to point in.

```
set rotation style left-right ▼
```

It is a good idea to set the rotation style to "left-right" so your sprites don't turn upside down when they move to the left.

Look at this quick help coordinate map if you get confused with the directions for up / down / left / right.

↑   ← - x + →

+   (0.0

y
-

↓

6. Changing Costumes – Celebrity Dress Up

Brad Pitt
from Wikipedia

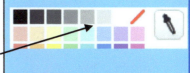

1. Find a celebrity image online and import it into the stage background of Scratch (or use a camera to take a picture of yourself!).

2. Erase the background in the paint editor. You can use the eraser tool (changing sizes helps). If the background is a solid color, you can use the paint tool to paint in "transparency" (the box with a red line across it).

3. <u>Duplicate</u> the entire sprite. (click on the "copy" button or use the stamp tool).

4. Choose a feature to change. The eyes are an easy one to start with. Erase everything except the eyes on the second sprite. (Use the select tool to outline the part you want to keep then press Shift-Delete (or Shift-Backspace) to delete everything else!)

5. Go to "costumes" and copy the image, leaving one "good" image.

6. Change the feature (eye color, nose size, etc) in the copy. You can draw over it or "import" another image from within the Paint Editor to add to it.

7. Build the code shown in the Scripts Area.

8. Make at least 2 changes to at least 4 features (hair, eyes, nose, ears, mustache).

when this sprite clicked
next costume

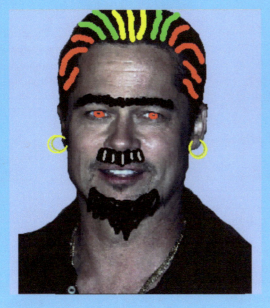

brad-pitt-...   brad-pitt-...   brad-pitt-...   brad-pitt-...

Project Notes:
- This is <u>not</u> an assignment to simply graffiti a picture. You should be able to click on the features to return to the original image.
- Neither is this an assignment meant to put down or disparage a celebrity or other students.
- Do not use someone's picture from your class without their permission.
- Do not make the picture gruesome, bloody, or hateful in any way. ☺

7. Changing Costumes – Autobiography Collage

1. Create a collage about 6 things that are an important part of your life. Ideas include:
   - your picture, family, pets, hobbies, sports, school, friends
   - favorite movies, books, singers, foods, sports, games, actors
   - colleges you want to attend, places you want to live, or jobs you want to have in the future

2. Find two (2) images online that represent whatever your important thing is and save them to your desktop. Make sure you leave the ".gif", ".jpg", or ".png" suffixes on the end, otherwise Scratch won't be able to "see" them as images. (You can also create your own sprite using the Text tool to type in a quote or name.)

3. The first costume is a "thumbnail" or small image. Load it in using the "Upload sprite from file" icon.

4. Now add the second image as another costume for the first one by using the "Upload costume from file" icon.

5. Create the two scripts of code shown. The first sets the starting costume, location, and size. When clicked, the second script tells the sprite to move to the middle of the stage (0,0), switch to the second costume, wait, the switch and move back.

6. Repeat Steps 3-5 for your other important things.

Favorite Quote

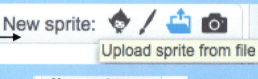

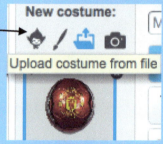

This code sets the original costume, location, and size for each sprite.

```
when [flag] clicked
switch costume to lord-of-the-ring
go to x: 0 y: 90
set size to 33 %
```

Manchester_... 254x283
lord-of-the-ring 480x323
Screen Shot ... 121x149
football-wallpap 480x300
LOTR 480x237
bl 480x270

Shown above are the two costumes for three of the sprites in the example collage.

- You can also make the sprite tilt, spin, talk, change color, etc. to jazz up your presentation.

- You can save time by dragging a script to another sprite. Scratch will copy it over for you!

This code tells the sprite to…
- go in front of everything else
- glide to the center of the stage (0,0)
- grow to normal size
- switch costumes
- wait 3 seconds
- reset the size, switch back, and go back to the first location

```
when this sprite clicked
go to front
glide 1 secs to x: 0 y: 0
set size to 100 %
switch costume to LOTR
wait 3 secs
set size to 33 %
next costume
glide 1 secs to x: 0 y: 90
```

8. Using Instruments – Making Music

1. Import a sprite and modify it (or draw your own) so that you have two costumes, one "singing" (with the mouth open) and one not singing (with the mouth closed).

2. Create the code shown for the first sprite.

3. After you create your first "singer", duplicate it (which also copies all the code associated with it).

4. Change the "when 'a' key pressed" to the next key on the keyboard. It seems to work best to use the keys in one row (A-S-D-F-G-H-J) to go through one octave, or series of 8 notes.

5. You can use different instruments for each key, or keep them all set the same.

6. Change the "play note '60' …" to the next note on the piano keyboard.

7. Add an insteresting background on the Stage.

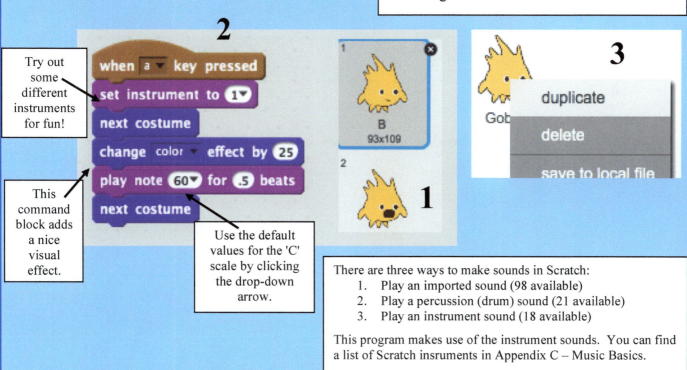

Try out some different instruments for fun!

This command block adds a nice visual effect.

Use the default values for the 'C' scale by clicking the drop-down arrow.

There are three ways to make sounds in Scratch:
1. Play an imported sound (98 available)
2. Play a percussion (drum) sound (21 available)
3. Play an instrument sound (18 available)

This program makes use of the instrument sounds. You can find a list of Scratch insruments in Appendix C – Music Basics.

9. Drawing Commands – Name Art

1. Create a sprite with your first initial. You can use the Text tool, draw your letter with the paintbrush, or load an image in that you found online.

2. Make all of the code for your first letter, then duplicate that sprite and change the costume for your other initials (you can also make your entire first name if you want).

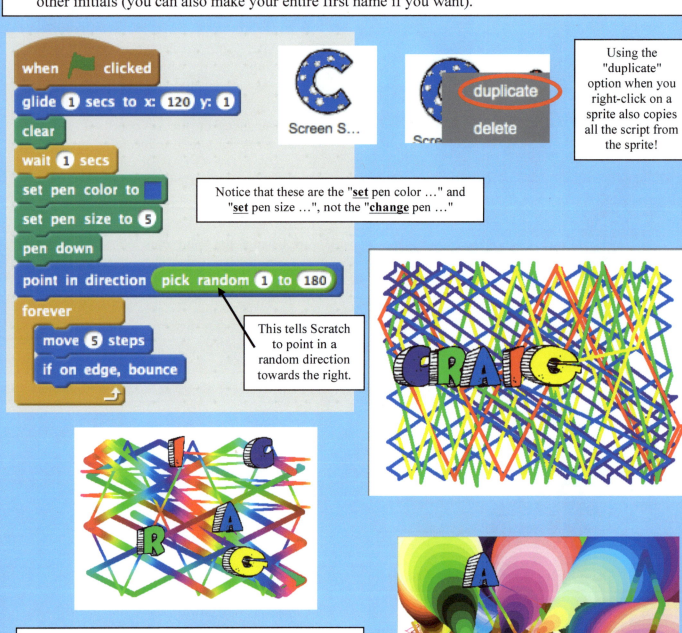

when 🏳 clicked
glide **1** secs to x: **120** y: **1**
clear
wait **1** secs
set pen color to ▉
set pen size to **5**
pen down
point in direction (pick random **1** to **180**)
forever
  move **5** steps
  if on edge, bounce

Screen S...

duplicate
delete

Screen S...

Using the "duplicate" option when you right-click on a sprite also copies all the script from the sprite!

Notice that these are the "**set** pen color …" and "**set** pen size …", not the "**change** pen …"

This tells Scratch to point in a random direction towards the right.

You can get interesting effects by trying some of these pen command blocks in the "forever" loop.

1. set pen color to (y position)   = rainbows

2. set pen size to (x position)   = blobs

3. stamp   = interesting lines

10. Using Hide and Show – Hidden Objects

1. Choose a background to work with. The one shown is called "room1" from the "Indoors" section. You can also search online for a "hidden object background".

2. Import pictures to hide around the room (like the baseball). You can also duplicate the original background and cut out an image (like the guitar). You should have at least 10 hidden objects.

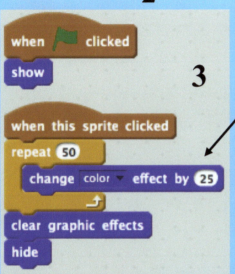

3. Add the code. It basically tells the object to show up at the start, blink if clicked on, then disappear. (If your objects are only black and white, then they won't change color with this code!)

4. Create a variable to count the objects as they are found. It is important to make variables "for all sprites", never "for this sprite only".

5. Add the "set found to 0" and "change found by 1" to the hidden items.

6. Create the code that checks to see if all the items have been found. When they are all found (found = 10), say "All done!!". Only one of the items needs these blocks of code.

To copy of an item from your backdrop, duplicate the backdrop costume, then drag it down to a sprite. Scratch will add it as a sprite costume.

You can also find some good hidden object backgrounds online.

11. Using Conditionals – Maze

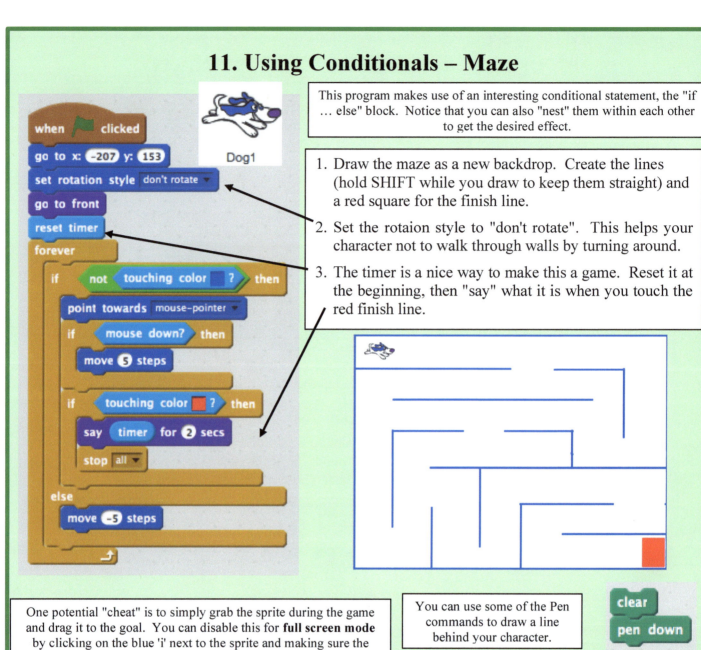

This program makes use of an interesting conditional statement, the "if … else" block. Notice that you can also "nest" them within each other to get the desired effect.

1. Draw the maze as a new backdrop. Create the lines (hold SHIFT while you draw to keep them straight) and a red square for the finish line.

2. Set the rotaion style to "don't rotate". This helps your character not to walk through walls by turning around.

3. The timer is a nice way to make this a game. Reset it at the beginning, then "say" what it is when you touch the red finish line.

One potential "cheat" is to simply grab the sprite during the game and drag it to the goal. You can disable this for **full screen mode** by clicking on the blue 'i' next to the sprite and making sure the "can drag in player" box is **unchecked**.

You can use some of the Pen commands to draw a line behind your character.

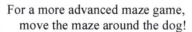

For a more advanced maze game, move the maze around the dog!

1. Make your maze larger (150% is the max) so that most of it is off the screen.

2. Add a "black out" sprite (black screen with a hole in the middle) so you can't see the maze as well,

3. Control the movement of the maze sprite with arrow keys and reverse the directions - so for the dog to "move" right, the maze would move to the left.

12. Platform Game

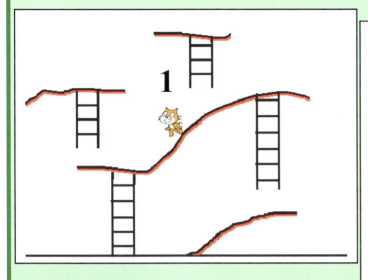

1. Draw a series of platforms as a sprite (<u>not on the stage</u>). Include ladders to climb and edges to drop from. You can also add in ropes, vines, etc.
2. Add a thin layer of another color (I used red) under each platform (this is to make the cat climb when it walks up or down the hills).
3. Make the cat move left – right with the arrow keys.
4. Make the cat climb when pressing up **and** touching a ladder (sprite 2 on my program).
5. Make the cat fall if not touching the platform or ladder.
6. Make the cat move up when touching the color red (or whichever color you used in step 2).

```
when [green flag] clicked
forever
  if < touching Sprite2 ? > then
    if < key [up arrow] pressed? > then
      change y by (5)
      next costume                    4
  else
    change y by (-3)                   5
```

```
when [green flag] clicked
forever
  if < key [right arrow] pressed? > then
    point in direction (90)
    change x by (5)                    3
    next costume
  if < key [left arrow] pressed? > then
    point in direction (-90)
    change x by (-5)
    next costume
```

```
when [green flag] clicked
forever                               6
  if < touching color [red] ? > then
    change y by (3)
```

Ideas to improve the game:
- Add a goal to reach or items to "pick up" around the screen.
- Duplicate the platform sprite, erase some of the platforms, and have it change costumes evey 2-3 seconds – this will simulate disappearing platforms.
- Add a forest background and change the ladders into vines.
- Modify the "up arrow" code so that the cat can jump up, even if not touching the ladders.
- Add sounds for falling or loop a sound track for background music.

13. Simulating Gravity – Jumping Cat

The goal of this game is to reach the red finish line while jumping over the rolling ball.

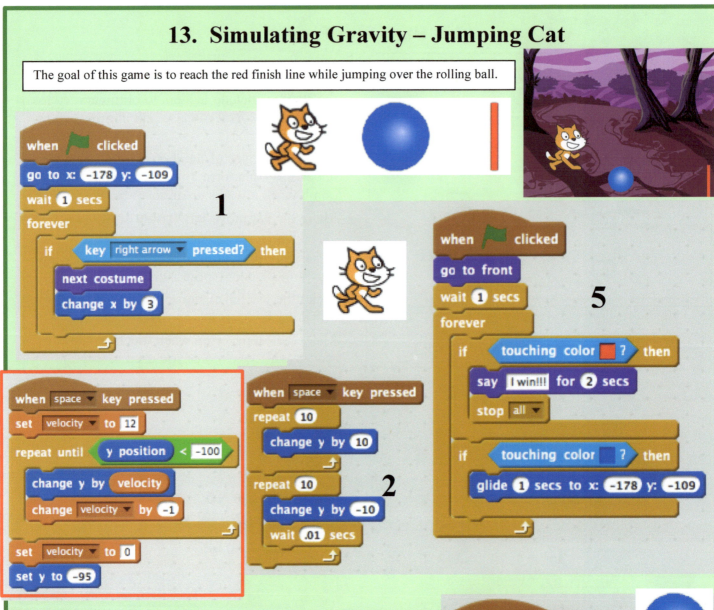

1
```
when 🏳 clicked
go to x: -178 y: -109
wait 1 secs
forever
    if  key right arrow pressed? then
        next costume
        change x by 3
```

```
when space key pressed
set velocity to 12
repeat until  y position < -100
    change y by velocity
    change velocity by -1
set velocity to 0
set y to -95
```

2
```
when space key pressed
repeat 10
    change y by 10
repeat 10
    change y by -10
    wait .01 secs
```

5
```
when 🏳 clicked
go to front
wait 1 secs
forever
    if  touching color 🟥 ? then
        say I win!!! for 2 secs
        stop all
    if  touching color 🟦 ? then
        glide 1 secs to x: -178 y: -109
```

3
4
```
when 🏳 clicked
repeat 10
    go to x: 218 y: -139
    show
    repeat 50
        turn ↻ 15 degrees
        change x by -10
    hide
    wait  pick random 1 to 3 secs
```

1. Create the code for the cat to start in the lower left corner and move to the right with the right arrow key. Adding the "next costume" code makes it look like it is running.

2. Add the "jumping" code. You can modify the numbers to change the jump. Notice that the "when space key pressed" allows the code to be used over and over without a "forever" loop.   An alternate jumping code is shown (outlined in red) in case you want the "jump" to be more realistic.

3. Draw a ball. Remember to hold "shift" to make a perfect circle. Fill it with a two color, circular blend to look 3D.

4. Add the code to make the ball roll. We are using "change x by -10" instead of "move -10 steps" so we can make the ball look like it's rolling.

5. Create the red finish line and add the winning code (touching color red) and the bounce back code (touching color blue).

14. Asking Questions – Quiz Show

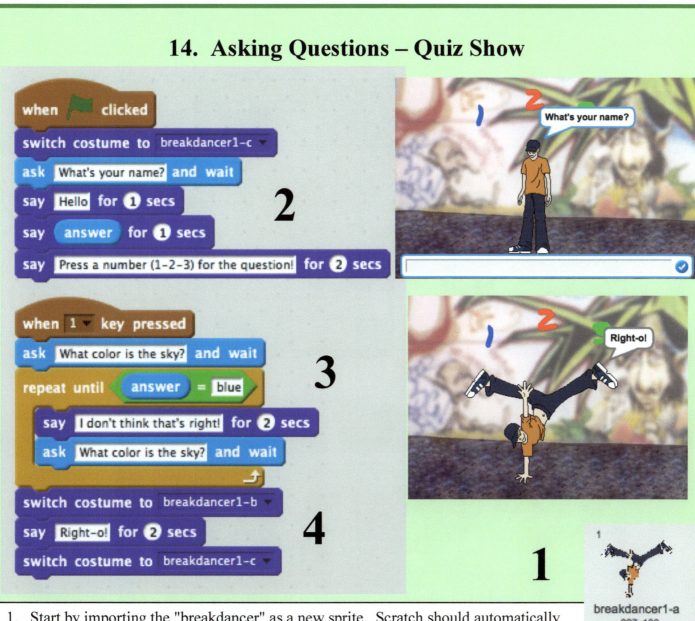

```
when [flag] clicked
switch costume to breakdancer1-c
ask What's your name? and wait
say Hello for 1 secs
say (answer) for 1 secs
say Press a number (1-2-3) for the question! for 2 secs
```

2

```
when 1 key pressed
ask What color is the sky? and wait
repeat until < (answer) = blue >
    say I don't think that's right! for 2 secs
    ask What color is the sky? and wait
switch costume to breakdancer1-b
say Right-o! for 2 secs
switch costume to breakdancer1-c
```

3

4

1

1. Start by importing the "breakdancer" as a new sprite. Scratch should automatically import his other 2 costumes. If not, import them as costumes.

2. Build the intro code. Notice that the "answer" variable goes into the "say" code.

3. Build the code for question 1. (You can use the text tool to put it right on the backdrop or add the numbers 1, 2, and 3 as a sprite - but the code needs to stay on the breakdancer.)

4. Have the breakdancer change to a different costume for each different question.

5. Duplicate the question code to create numbers 2 and 3 (right-click or control-click on the top code block to duplicate). Notice that you can use an "or" block to check for two similar answers.

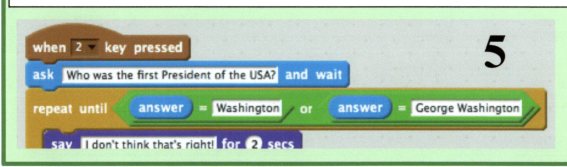

```
when 2 key pressed
ask Who was the first President of the USA? and wait
repeat until < (answer) = Washington or (answer) = George Washington >
    say I don't think that's right! for 2 secs
```

5

15. Pong

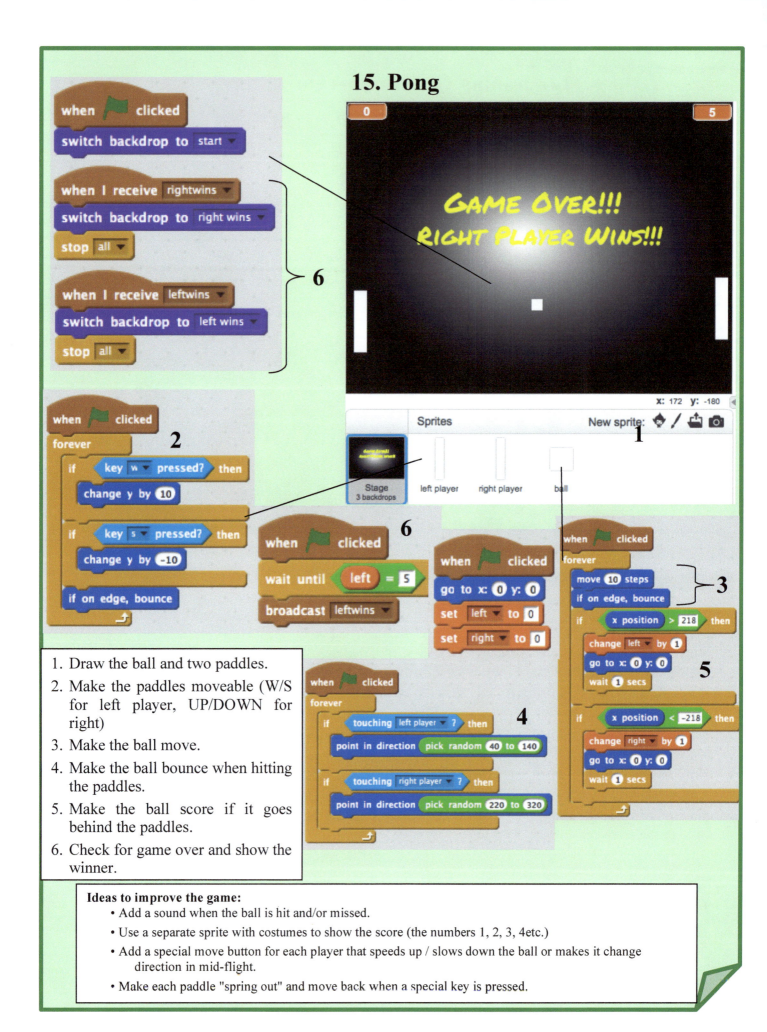

when 🚩 clicked
switch backdrop to start ▼

when I receive rightwins ▼
switch backdrop to right wins ▼
stop all ▼

when I receive leftwins ▼
switch backdrop to left wins ▼
stop all ▼

6

when 🚩 clicked
forever
  if   key w ▼ pressed?   then
    change y by 10
  if   key s ▼ pressed?   then
    change y by -10
  if on edge, bounce

2

when 🚩 clicked
wait until (left = 5)
broadcast leftwins ▼

6

when 🚩 clicked
go to x: 0 y: 0
set left ▼ to 0
set right ▼ to 0

when 🚩 clicked
forever
  if   touching left player ▼ ?   then
    point in direction pick random 40 to 140
  if   touching right player ▼ ?   then
    point in direction pick random 220 to 320

4

when 🚩 clicked
forever
  move 10 steps
  if on edge, bounce

3

  if   x position > 218   then
    change left ▼ by 1
    go to x: 0 y: 0
    wait 1 secs

5

  if   x position < -218   then
    change right ▼ by 1
    go to x: 0 y: 0
    wait 1 secs

Sprites — New sprite:
Stage 3 backdrops — left player — right player — ball

x: 172 y: -180

1. Draw the ball and two paddles.
2. Make the paddles moveable (W/S for left player, UP/DOWN for right)
3. Make the ball move.
4. Make the ball bounce when hitting the paddles.
5. Make the ball score if it goes behind the paddles.
6. Check for game over and show the winner.

Ideas to improve the game:
- Add a sound when the ball is hit and/or missed.
- Use a separate sprite with costumes to show the score (the numbers 1, 2, 3, 4etc.)
- Add a special move button for each player that speeds up / slows down the ball or makes it change direction in mid-flight.
- Make each paddle "spring out" and move back when a special key is pressed.

16. Using a Missile – Hit the Target

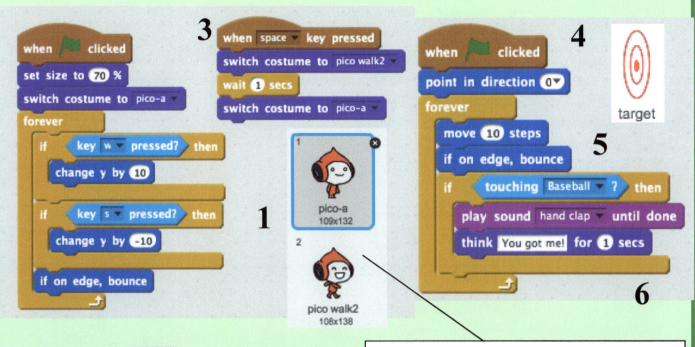

3

```
when space key pressed
switch costume to pico walk2
wait 1 secs
switch costume to pico-a
```

```
when [flag] clicked
set size to 70 %
switch costume to pico-a
forever
    if  key w pressed?  then
        change y by 10
    if  key s pressed?  then
        change y by -10
    if on edge, bounce
```

1

```
1
pico-a
109x132
2
pico walk2
108x138
```

4

target

5

```
when [flag] clicked
point in direction 0
forever
    move 10 steps
    if on edge, bounce
    if  touching Baseball ?  then
        play sound hand clap until done
        think You got me! for 1 secs
```

6

Baseball

2

```
when space key pressed
go to player
show
glide 0.5 secs to x: 240 y: y position of player
hide
```

```
when [flag] clicked
set size to 35 %
hide
```

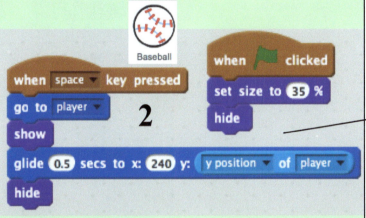

Ideas to improve the game:
- Add a background
- Add a score (place the "change score by 1" variable block in the "if touching ball" loop)
- Make the target "explode" when hit by switching costumes
- Add an extra target
- Add blocking pieces that also move up and down to shield the target.
- Make this a "themed" game – inport sprites from online for Star Wars, Sponge Bob, Transformers, etc.

1. Import the two "Pico" costumes. Make him move up and down with the arrow keys.

2. Import the ball. When the space key is pressed, make it go to Pico, appear, and fly across the screen. Use the "y position of …" block from the Sensing drawer so that the ball flies straight across the screen from whichever height Pico is curently at.

3. Make Pico switch costumes when the ball is "thrown" (the "space" key is pressed).

4. Draw a target. It's basically a large red oval around a smaller red oval with white painted in between. The key idea here is to **set its rotation to "don't rotate"** so that it doesn't turn sideways when it bounces up and down.

5. Make it point up initially and then move up and down forever.

6. Add in an "if touching ball" code block to see when it gets hit. You'll need to import the "hand clap" sound. Notice that this stops the target from moving when it gets hit because it is in the same loop as the movement code.

17. Intermediate Art – Recreate a Landscape

1. Choose a landscape image to recreate using Scratch's Paint Editor. You can find 10 free landscapes at **http://bit.ly/I2Vyrg** (capitalization counts!) or you can search for your own online using the search terms "free landscape background". You want an image that is large (at least 900 x 900) for best resolution in Scratch.

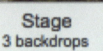

2. Import the original landscape image as the backdrop and paint your image as a second backdrop.

   - Your landscape should recreate the basic colors, shapes, shadows and (when possible) textures of the original image.

   - Start by outlining the different colored areas with the paintbrush tool. You want to mimic the general outline – it doesn't have to be perfect!

   - The amount of detail you include is up to you, but you will find different paintbrush sizes and using blended (or gradient) fills extremely useful.

3. Use the code shown to switch between the two as you work (or view the original image as you paint).

```
when space ▼ key pressed
next backdrop
```

You can modify the line width and use blended fills to recreate the natural colors.

4. When finished with your artistic recreation, you should add your name (at least initials) using the Text Tool in the Paint Editor.

CMW, NMS, 2014

5. Finally, save a picture of your artwork by right-clicking (or control-clicking) on the costume and choosing "save to local file"). You can then print this saved image from any image preview program.

18. Asteroids

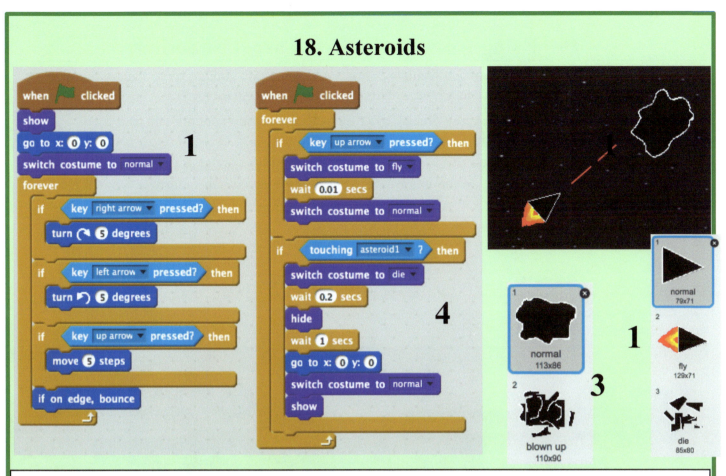

1. Start by drawing the 3 ship views, then add the movement codes. You can use the Select Tool to make the ship look "blown up". Notice the ship rotates left/right and only moves forward.

2. Create the "laser". When the fire key is pressed, it should go to the ship, point in the direction the ship is headed, show up and move until it hits the edge or the asteroid.

3. Create the 2 views of the asteroid. Make the asteroid show up in a random position, point in a random direction, and move around the stage until it hits the ship or is hit by the laser.

4. Add in the ship firing thrusters and blowing up.

```
when space key pressed
go to ship
point in direction (direction of ship)
show
repeat until (touching asteroid1 ?)
    if (touching edge ?) then
        wait .02 secs
        hide
        stop this script
    move 6 steps
hide
```
2

```
when green flag clicked
hide
```

```
when green flag clicked
forever
    switch costume to normal
    go to x: (pick random -200 to 200) y: (pick random -200 to 200)
    show
    point in direction (pick random 1 to 360)
    move 10 steps
    repeat until (touching ship ? or touching laser ?)
        move 3 steps
        if on edge, bounce
    switch costume to blown up
    wait 0.2 secs
    hide
    wait 1 secs
```
3

Additional ideas are to add sounds, more asteroids, more lasers, a black hole, an enemy ship, a score, etc.

19. Using Animated Gifs – Target Shooting

Gifs are one of the most popular image formats online. Animated gifs contain more than one image (or costume) and switch between them in a loop, creating the illusion of a small movie.

1. Download the animated gif (**http://bit.ly/He2wLU** capitalizaion counts!) or search online for "animated_DOVE.gif".

2. Import it from the new costumes tab and check to see that all of the costumes load into Scratch (make sure you leave the ".gif" suffix on the end of the name when you save it, otherwise Scratch may not recognize it as a picture file!).

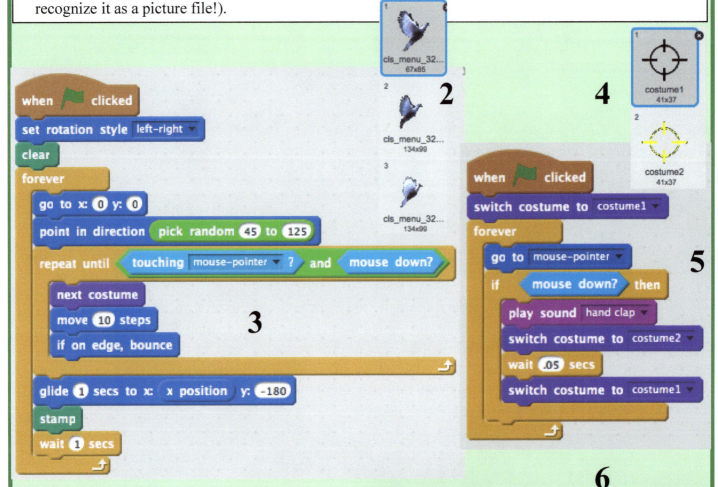

3. Create the code to make the bird move and change costumes until "shot" (mouse down and touching mouse pointer).

4. Draw the first "sight" costume. Make sure to leave the middle open! Then duplicate it and change the color of the second costume (yellow works well).

5. Add the code to make the sight change and play the "hand-clap" sound when the mouse is clicked.

6. Finally, add in an appropriate background.

20. Using Layers – Sniper Game

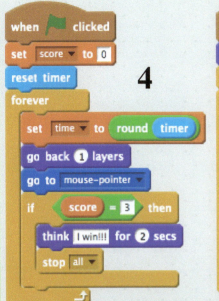

4

2

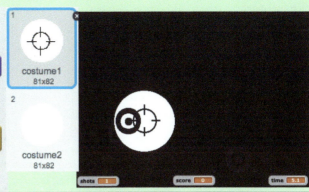

1. Start by making the stage black.

2. Next, draw the sight sprite: it is a filled white circle with a black target sight over it.

3. Make the next costume a solid white circle.

4. Add the code to make it follow the mouse-pointer and change costumes when you click.

There are a total of four sprites, but the three targets are all the same. Make the first target the way you want, then duplicate it to get the others.

5. Next draw the first target sprite.

6. Duplicate it and add a dart hitting the target, then make a third costume of the target breaking up.

7. Add the code to make it show up in a random location and cycle through it's costumes when it gets hit.

8. Duplicate the target sprite twice to get the three targets you need.

7

5

6

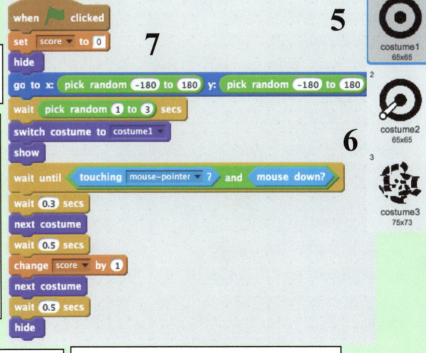

go back 1 layers

Key Block

This block keeps the "sight" always behind the targets, letting the black targets show on the white circle behind

There are three variables in this program: shots (how many you have taken), score (how many you have hit), and time (how long it takes you). Checking the box next to them will make them show on the stage. Notice that the "time" variable ("4" above) is the timer rounded to a whole number.

✓ **score**

✓ **shots**

✓ **time**

There are three layers to this program: the black targets in front of the white sight with the black background in back.

21. Using Instruments – Create-a-Song

Scratch allows both instrument and drum (percussion) sounds. Ths instruments are accessed by first setting the instrument and then playing a note for a number of beats. Appendix B contains a list of the instrument and drum types available (Scratch 2 has fewer choices than Scratch 1.4, but they seem to work much better!). Most music that we commonly hear today is played with four (4) beats per measure. So a normal length for a note would be 1 beat – the higher the number, the longer the note is held.

```
set instrument to (1▾)
play note (60▾) for (0.5) beats
```

```
set tempo to (60) bpm
```

```
play note (60▾) for (0.5) beats
```

You may also find it helpful to change the tempo (or speed) of the song. The default tempo is 60 bpm (beats per minute) which makes 1 beat last for 1 second. The higher the tempo, the shorter the length of each beat and the faster the song.

Here are some example songs to program. Create the code, then see which ones you recognize!

Note numbers
(72) High C
(71) B
(69) A
(67) G
(65) F
(64) E
(62) D
(60) Middle C
(59) B
(57) A
(55) G
(53) F
(52) E
(50) D
(48) Low C

```
when a ▾ key pressed
set tempo to (80) bpm
set instrument to (15▾)
play note (60▾) for (1) beats
play note (67▾) for (1) beats
play note (65▾) for (0.3) beats
play note (64▾) for (0.3) beats
play note (62▾) for (0.3) beats
play note (72▾) for (1) beats
play note (60▾) for (1) beats
play note (65▾) for (0.3) beats
play note (64▾) for (0.3) beats
play note (62▾) for (0.3) beats
play note (72▾) for (1) beats
play note (60▾) for (1) beats
play note (65▾) for (0.3) beats
play note (64▾) for (0.3) beats
play note (65▾) for (0.3) beats
play note (62▾) for (2) beats
```

```
when b ▾ key pressed
set tempo to (60) bpm
set instrument to (4▾)
play note (69▾) for (0.3) beats
rest for (0.3) beats
play note (62▾) for (0.3) beats
rest for (0.5) beats
play note (72▾) for (0.3) beats
rest for (0.15) beats
play note (69▾) for (0.2) beats
rest for (0.08) beats
play note (67▾) for (0.3) beats
rest for (0.2) beats
play note (60▾) for (0.3) beats
rest for (0.2) beats
```

```
when c ▾ key pressed
set tempo to (100) bpm
set instrument to (5▾)
play note (65▾) for (1) beats
play note (62▾) for (0.5) beats
play note (58▾) for (1) beats
play note (62▾) for (1) beats
play note (65▾) for (1) beats
play note (70▾) for (3) beats
```

```
when d ▾ key pressed
set tempo to (100) bpm
set instrument to (10▾)
play note (72▾) for (1.25) beats
play note (71▾) for (1.25) beats
play note (69▾) for (0.5) beats
play note (67▾) for (2) beats
play note (65▾) for (0.75) beats
play note (64▾) for (1.5) beats
play note (62▾) for (1.5) beats
play note (60▾) for (2) beats
```

For an extra challenge, program a song that you know or finish one of the examples that are started above.

22. Pac-Man

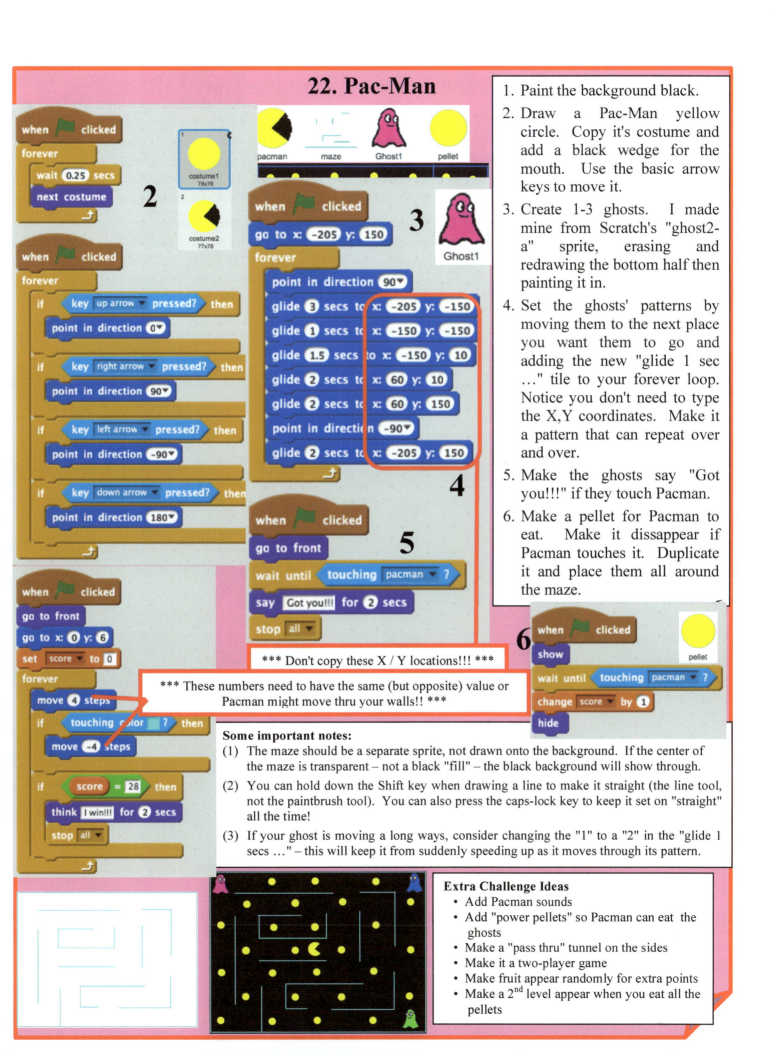

2

when [flag] clicked
forever
  wait 0.25 secs
  next costume

costume1 78x78
costume2 77x78

when [flag] clicked
forever
  if <key up arrow pressed?> then
    point in direction 0
  if <key right arrow pressed?> then
    point in direction 90
  if <key left arrow pressed?> then
    point in direction -90
  if <key down arrow pressed?> then
    point in direction 180

when [flag] clicked
go to front
go to x: 0 y: 6
set score to 0
forever
  move 4 steps
  if <touching color [ ]?> then
    move -4 steps
  if <score = 28> then
    think [I win!!!] for 2 secs
    stop all

pacman   maze   Ghost1   pellet

when [flag] clicked
go to x: -205 y: 150
forever
  point in direction 90
  glide 3 secs to x: -205 y: -150
  glide 1 secs to x: -150 y: -150
  glide 1.5 secs to x: -150 y: 10
  glide 2 secs to x: 60 y: 10
  glide 2 secs to x: 60 y: 150
  point in direction -90
  glide 2 secs to x: -205 y: 150

3

Ghost1

4

when [flag] clicked
go to front
wait until <touching pacman?>
say [Got you!!!] for 2 secs
stop all

5

*** Don't copy these X / Y locations!!! ***

*** These numbers need to have the same (but opposite) value or Pacman might move thru your walls!! ***

6

when [flag] clicked
show
wait until <touching pacman?>
change score by 1
hide

pellet

Instructions (right column)

1. Paint the background black.
2. Draw a Pac-Man yellow circle. Copy it's costume and add a black wedge for the mouth. Use the basic arrow keys to move it.
3. Create 1-3 ghosts. I made mine from Scratch's "ghost2-a" sprite, erasing and redrawing the bottom half then painting it in.
4. Set the ghosts' patterns by moving them to the next place you want them to go and adding the new "glide 1 sec …" tile to your forever loop. Notice you don't need to type the X,Y coordinates. Make it a pattern that can repeat over and over.
5. Make the ghosts say "Got you!!!" if they touch Pacman.
6. Make a pellet for Pacman to eat. Make it dissappear if Pacman touches it. Duplicate it and place them all around the maze.

Some important notes:
(1) The maze should be a separate sprite, not drawn onto the background. If the center of the maze is transparent – not a black "fill" – the black background will show through.
(2) You can hold down the Shift key when drawing a line to make it straight (the line tool, not the paintbrush tool). You can also press the caps-lock key to keep it set on "straight" all the time!
(3) If your ghost is moving a long ways, consider changing the "1" to a "2" in the "glide 1 secs …" – this will keep it from suddenly speeding up as it moves through its pattern.

Extra Challenge Ideas
- Add Pacman sounds
- Add "power pellets" so Pacman can eat the ghosts
- Make a "pass thru" tunnel on the sides
- Make it a two-player game
- Make fruit appear randomly for extra points
- Make a 2nd level appear when you eat all the pellets

23. Using Scrolling Backgrounds – Cat Walk

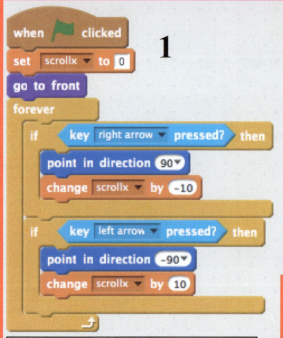

1. Create the movement code for the cat. Notice that the arrow keys don't actually move the cat, they just change the variable, "scrollx". Also, they change it in the opposite way, so to give the appearance of moving right, the variable (and backdrop) has to move left.

2. Here's the tricky part: Scratch 2 won't let you (easily) load a backdrop as a sprite, so we need to trick it into doing that. Pick out any sprite from Scratch's files, then load the brick wall backdrop as a backdrop. Click the "backdrops" tab and drag the costume of the brick wall down to the sprite you loaded. Scratch should copy the brick wall into the sprite's costumes.

Create the variable "scrollx" for "all sprites"!!!

3. Create the code for the backdrop to move. Try it out.

4. This works well for only one background (wall), but it's nice to add more. Duplicate your wall and change the code as shown. Since the stage is 480 pixels wide, the "+470" moves the next wall over to the right.

5. Add as many walls as you want, adding 470 more pixels each time.

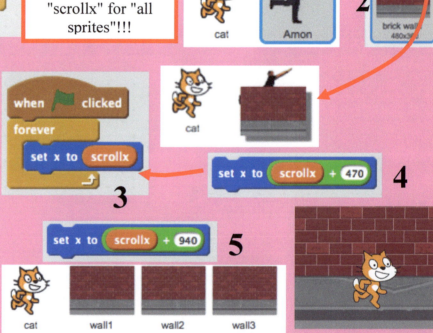

* You can also use a multiplication block to add more walls if you get tired of figuring it out yourself:

* You may need to adjust the "470" to a lower or higher number to reduce flickering at the edges.

* You can increase the realism of the scrolling by flipping each backdrop sprite horizontally so their edges match up more closely.

* If this overtaxes your computer's graphics card, try just scrolling the lower half of a backdrop and use a static or fixed backdrop for the upper backround.

* Finally, make a few additions: have the cat change costumes to walk, add jumping, create a finish line, make some objects to avoid, add a timer, have the backdrops hide until they are supposed to show up. Have some fun with this!!

24. Simulating 3D – Desert Walk

Palmtree   Rocks

2

1. Import a background on the stage. Use the paintbrush and stamp tools to erase any images in the foreground (like the cacti above), including color differences (like the lighter sand above).

2. Import a sprite that fits the backdrop. I used a palm tree and the rocks. Set the size and location where you want them to begin

3. Create the code to change their size and location as you move toward or away from them.

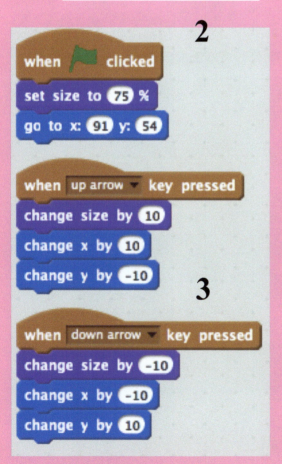

3

25. Using the Pen Commands – Etch-a-Sketch Art

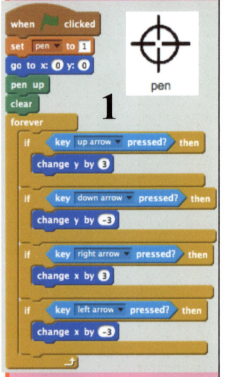

1

There are 6 basic ideas in this program. All codes except #6 (color reminder) and #7 (backdrop color) go on the pen sprite.

1. Pen movement is controlled by the arrow keys.

2. The line colors can be changed by pressing a color key.

3. The space key acts as a switch, toggling the pen up (-1) or down (1) by multiplying the variable "pen" by -1.

4. The 'a' and 'z' keys make the pen wider or narrower. The pen width can't go below 1.

5. The 'c' key asks if they want to clear the screen

6. The 'h' key shows a sprite reminding the user which colors are available.

7. The 'x' key changes between the colors of stage backdrops.

3

This code uses the variable 'pen' as a switch by multiplying by -1 each time the space key is pressed. <u>It has to be set to '1' at the start or it won't work.</u>

4

2

7

5

The code to the right goes on a separate sprite. You can use the text tool to type out the first letter of the available colors. I used the colors of the rainbow, black, white, pink, and brown.

6

r-o-y-g-b-i-v-l-w-p-n

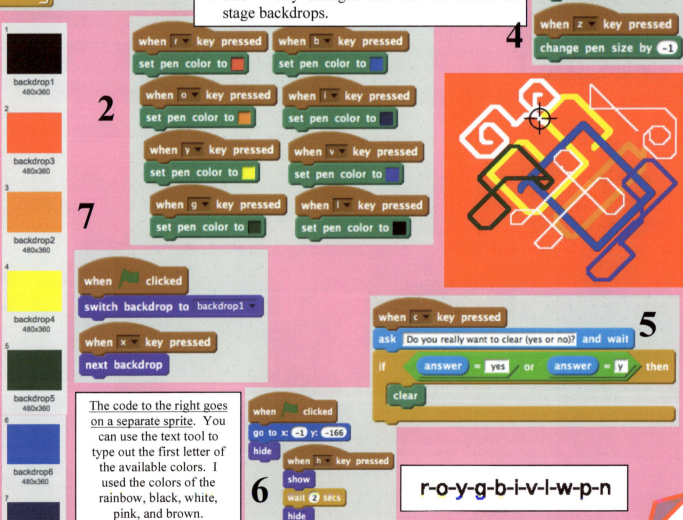

26. Using Lists – Number Guessing Game

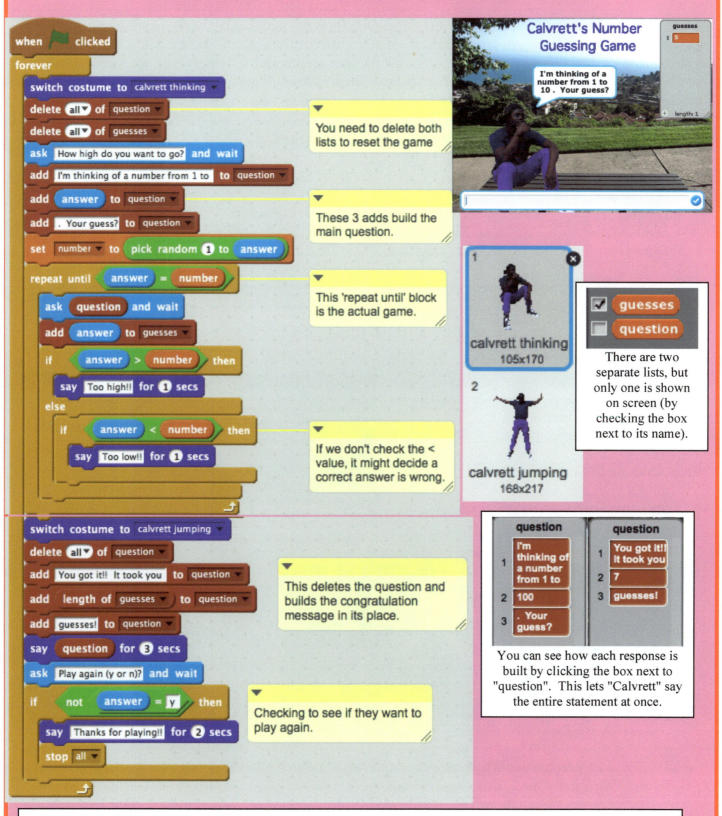

Calvrett's Number Guessing Game

I'm thinking of a number from 1 to 10 . Your guess?

```
when [green flag] clicked
forever
    switch costume to calvrett thinking
    delete (all) of question
    delete (all) of guesses
    ask [How high do you want to go?] and wait
    add [I'm thinking of a number from 1 to] to question
    add (answer) to question
    add [. Your guess?] to question
    set number to (pick random (1) to (answer))
    repeat until <(answer) = (number)>
        ask (question) and wait
        add (answer) to guesses
        if <(answer) > (number)> then
            say [Too high!!] for (1) secs
        else
            if <(answer) < (number)> then
                say [Too low!!] for (1) secs
```

You need to delete both lists to reset the game

These 3 adds build the main question.

This 'repeat until' block is the actual game.

If we don't check the < value, it might decide a correct answer is wrong.

There are two separate lists, but only one is shown on screen (by checking the box next to its name).

calvrett thinking 105x170

calvrett jumping 168x217

guesses
question

```
    switch costume to calvrett jumping
    delete (all) of question
    add [You got it!! It took you] to question
    add (length of guesses) to question
    add [guesses!] to question
    say (question) for (3) secs
    ask [Play again (y or n)?] and wait
    if <not <(answer) = [y]>> then
        say [Thanks for playing!!] for (2) secs
        stop (all)
```

This deletes the question and builds the congratulation message in its place.

Checking to see if they want to play again.

question		question	
1	I'm thinking of a number from 1 to	1	You got it!! It took you
2	100	2	7
3	. Your guess?	3	guesses!

You can see how each response is built by clicking the box next to "question". This lets "Calvrett" say the entire statement at once.

- You don't have to use "Calvrett" for the questioner – you could use a picture of your face with different "thoughtful" expressions.
- This program makes use of several different "key blocks": asking questions, making lists, making a variable, random numbers, and conditional checking (if… loops).
- I would start with the actual game code (in the middle of the program) then add the lists once it is working correctly.

27. Create Your Own Retro Game

Recreate a famous retro game ("retro" meaning from the recent past). You may use online images and sounds. Your game does not have to recreate the entire original game, but it should closely approximate the original game play. This should be your programming entirely and not simply someone else's work that you modify. Fill in the "Retro Game Planning" page and get the teacher's approval before you start programming. Have fun!!

15 Suggested "Retro" Games to Program

1. Adventure
2. Breakout
3. DigDug
4. DonkeyKong
5. Duck Hunt

6. Frogger
7. Galaga
8. Jungle Hunt
9. Mario Brothers
10. Missile Command

11. Moon Patrol
12. Pitfall
13. Pole Position
14. Space Invaders
15. Tron (Light Cycles)

Some of these games can be viewed/played online at www.classicgamesarcade.com.

Frogger © Sega, image from Wikipedia

Free Online Resources

Free Sound Clips and Music Loops
http://www.partnersinrhyme.com

Free Older Game Images
http://www.retrogamezone.co.uk/

Free Animated Gifs
http://www.gifs.net/gif/
http://www.amazing-animations.com
http://www.gifanimations.com/

Super Mario Bros © Nintendo, image from Wikipedia

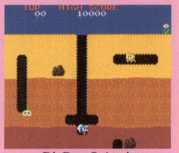

DigDug © Atari, image from Wikipedia

Space Invaders © Midway, image from Wikipedia

Pole Position © Atari, image from Wikipedia

Breakout © Atari, image from Wikipedia

Making these types of games is a great way to challenge students to program on their own but still give them established guidelines. By using a retro game they already have an idea of what the game should look like and how it should be played. Additionally, most older games have relatively simple gameplay and use 2D interfaces. Another good suggestion is to have them search for "screenshot" and the name of the game to find the backgrounds they need (if they don't want to make their own). Also, if a game is very complex, I usually let the students create just a part of it if necessary. This assignment usually takes 7-8 class days of work time.

28. Create Your Own Original Game

Create your own game. This may be based on another game, but it should not be exactly like another game. You may use online images and sounds or ones that you draw in Scratch. This should be your own planning and programming <u>entirely</u> and not simply someone else's programming that you modify. Fill in the "Original Game Planning" page and get the teacher's approval before you start programming. Have fun!!

The Seven Stages of Game Programming

Stage 1 Vision – get an idea in mind, don't start off too grand just keep it simple. (Sometimes the simplest games are the best!) Don't get bogged down in details (yet). Think of basic questions like will it go side-to-side, up and down, or just down?

Stage 2 Planning – make a list, a web diagram, and/or a drawing about your game idea. What What sprites will you need? Will you need to use any variables? What is the best way for the player to input control?

Stage 3 Programming – start filling in the code for each sprite. Save often and save as different versions (ie. game1, game2) in case you program yourself into a corner and want to go back. It helps to play and fix as you go. Remember to keep variables informative so you can easily remember what they stand for.

Stage 4 Evaluation – step back, play it, think about it again. Do you need to make it faster or slower? Is there an easier way to code it? Will the game make sense to someone else?

Stage 5 Outside Critique – have a friend play and get their opinion. Even though it's difficult, listen to them, listen to them, listen to them. What makes sense to you may be confusing to them!

Stage 6 Repeat Stages 3 through 5 until you are satisfied with your game.

Stage 7 Clean Up – add credits to your game and a Splash Screen to the start or end. Cleanup any cumbersome code. Rename the file with an interesting Game Title.

PPPPP

There is an old saying that really holds true in programming: Prior Planning Prevents Poor Performance. The more you plan out ahead of time, the less problems you will deal with during programming which means you will usually finish your game much more quickly and it will turn out more the way you want it. Since there are usually several ways to program the same thing, the structure or shape of your programming can set you up for an elegant game or a waste of code. I usually write out my ideas on paper first, then start coding on the computer after I have a broad picture. Whichever method you find works best for you remember, prior planning prevents poor performance. (It's even an example of alliteration, for your English language development!)

29. Real-World Challenge #1 – Office Security Lighting

Your programming company has been contacted by another company. They want you to design a computer program to help increase their office security by tying a series of lights to various doors. Their requirements are listed below. You can find their office diagram on the following webpage: `http://bit.ly/HKJASr` (capital letters count). Create a program in Scratch that satisfies their requirements.

Customer Requirements:
1. Green Light in Private Office to come on if the front door opens.
2. Yellow Light outside of Conference Room to come on if Conference Room door is closed.
3. Red Light in Reception to come on if the Private Office door closes.
4. Blue Light in Reception to come on if the Storage & Filing room door opens.
5. A buzzer to sound when the front door opens.
6. Add a push button on the reception desk to disable the security lights and buzzers.

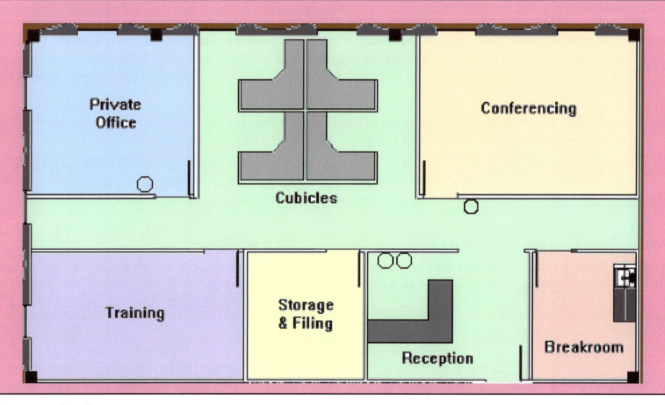

Programming Strategy:
a. Make the doors for each room "movable" (open – close) when clicked on.
b. Tie the required doors to the lights. Make sure you use the colors they requested.
c. Make the front door and Storage & Filing door self-closing (open, wait, then close on it's own).
d. Tie in a buzzer sound to the front door opening.
e. Add in a disable button on the reception desk that shuts off all the lights. One way is to use a variable switch (1*-1).

30. Real-World Challenge #2 – Debugging Bug Bounce

"When you get a first **entry-level programming** job you will most likely **not** be writing all new code yourself, but instead you will be **modifying and debugging existing code** (program maintenance). The only new code you might write is to make product enhancements to existing products. No one is going to sit you down at a computer and expect you to write an entirely new program all by yourself." ~ posted 6/23/11 by 'Ancient Dragon', a retired programmer at http://www.daniweb.com/software-development/cpp/threads/369511/1588290#post1588290

You have just been hired at a company that specializes in making games for children about bugs. Your first assignment is to debug ☺ an older program (called 'Bug Bounce') that they have received several complaints about. If you can't find and correct the errors in the programming code, they will have to pull the game from their website and issue refunds to all the families that have already purchased it!

The original vision for the game was to control a bug (butterfly) with the right and left arrow keys, making it fly back and forth along the blue / purple boundary, bouncing colored, bouncy balls off of its back until it reached a score of 20 when a "YOU WIN" message shows up. When the bug missed a bouncy ball, it was supposed to subtract from the score and make a laughing sound.

Download the program from **http://bit.ly/Gm2G2f** (capitilization counts!) or recreate it from the code shown below. Run it, then fix the 10 errors in the coding to address the top 10 complaints that have been received from irate parents.

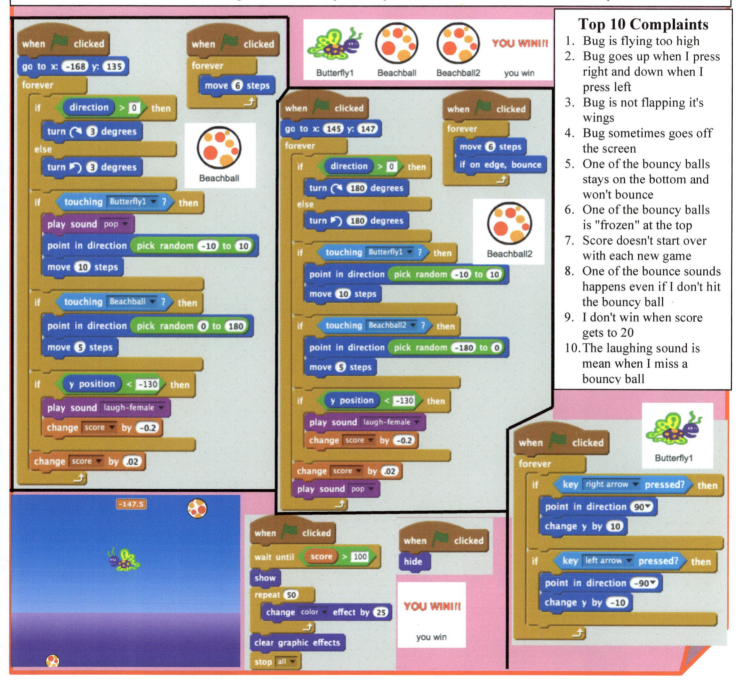

Top 10 Complaints
1. Bug is flying too high
2. Bug goes up when I press right and down when I press left
3. Bug is not flapping it's wings
4. Bug sometimes goes off the screen
5. One of the bouncy balls stays on the bottom and won't bounce
6. One of the bouncy balls is "frozen" at the top
7. Score doesn't start over with each new game
8. One of the bounce sounds happens even if I don't hit the bouncy ball
9. I don't win when score gets to 20
10. The laughing sound is mean when I miss a bouncy ball

Additional Worksheets

Scratch Reflection Sheet for _____

1. What was the most difficult part about this program?

2. What was the most fun or enjoyable part about this program?

3. Which programming block(s) was (were) the most critical to making the program function correctly?

4. What is one change or addition you made to the basic program you were given?

5. On the following scale, how difficult   1 – 2 – 3 – 4 –5 – 6 – 7 – 8 – 9 – 10
   was it to create this program: most   medium   most
                                             easy   difficult

----

Scratch Reflection Sheet for _____

1. What was the most difficult part about this program?

2. What was the most fun or enjoyable part about this program?

3. Which programming block(s) was (were) the most critical to making the program function correctly?

4. What is one change or addition you made to the basic program you were given?

5. On the following scale, how difficult   1 – 2 – 3 – 4 –5 – 6 – 7 – 8 – 9 – 10
   was it to create this program: most   medium   most
                                             easy   difficult

Scratch Retro Game Planning

Recreate a retro game. You may use online images and sounds. Your game does not have to recreate the entire original game, but it should closely approximate the original game play. This should be your programming entirely and not simply someone else's work that you modify. Have fun!!

Game Planning Sheet

Type of Game

Breakout	Dig-Dug	DonkeyKong	Frogger	Galaga
Jungle Hunt	Mario Brothers	Missle Command	Pole Position	Space Invaders

Type of Control   mouse pointer   keyboard   arrow-keys

Goal of Game   "You must ... _____

_____

_____

Sprite Images You Will Need from Online

Teacher's Initials [   ]

Sketch of Game Screen

Scratch Retro Game Review

1. Title of your game: _____

2. How difficult was it to program your game?   1 – 2 – 3 – 4 – 5 – 6 – 7 – 8 – 9 – 10
                                                           easy   okay   my brain hurts

3. How much is your game like the original?   1 – 2 – 3 – 4 – 5 – 6 – 7 – 8 – 9 – 10
                                          not at all   a little   exactly

4. What was the most challenging part of the programming for your game?

5. Did you draw your sprites on your own, use the Scratch ones or download them from the Internet?

6. If you were to start programming your game over, what would you do differently from the beginning?

Have someone else fill in the bottom portion of this review.

7. Game Reviewer First Name: _____

8. How **fun** was it to play this game?   1 – 2 – 3 – 4 – 5 – 6 – 7 – 8 – 9 – 10
                                 yawn   a little   Woohoo!

9. How **easy** was it to play this game?   1 – 2 – 3 – 4 – 5 – 6 – 7 – 8 – 9 – 10
                                 too easy   just right   too difficult

10. What is one positive comment you can make about this game?

11. What are two things you'd like to see changed about this game?

_____
(Game Reviewer Signature)

NAME _____

Scratch Original Game Planning

Create your own game. This may be based on another game, but it should not be exactly like another game. You may use online images and sounds. This should be your own planning and programming entirely and not simply someone else's work that you modify. Have fun!!

Game Planning Sheet

Goal of Game   "You must ... _____

_____

Type of Game

Animation / Story	Pseudo-3D	Art	Flying / Driving	Shooting
Scrolling	Platform	Sports	Quiz Game	_____

Type of Control   mouse pointer   keyboard   arrow-keys

Sprite Images You Will Need from Online

Teacher's Initials ☐

Sketch of Game Screen

Scratch Original Game Report

Title of game / story _____

Goal of game / Plot of story _____

_____

_____

Do you have a Start Screen?   YES - NO

Number of ...

      sprites:

      stage backgrounds:

      sounds:

      variables (including timer):

Can the user control the game / story? YES - NO   If YES, how? _____

_____

Which sprites did you get from the Internet?

Which sprites did you draw on your own?

How does the game / story end? _____

_____

What is the most interesting part of your game / story?

List 5 important control blocks you used in this program:

Have another person review your game / story

    Reviewer's Name _____

    What is one thing you liked about this game / story:

    What is one thing you like to see added to this game / story:

    On a scale of 5 to 10, how much do you like this game?

                       5 – 6 – 7 – 8 – 9 – 10

                not bad   greatest game ever

Scratch Online Program Review
WEBSITE: **scratch.mit.edu**

| **1** | Name of Game / Program:
Describe the Program: |

Ease of Play (1-hard to 10-easy):

What are two things you like:

What are two things you would change:

What are two programming blocks (tiles) you think they used to create this program:

| **2** | Name of Game / Program:
Describe the Program: |

Ease of Play (1-hard to 10-easy):

What are two things you like:

What are two things you would change:

What are two programming blocks (tiles) you think they used to create this program:

| **3** | Name of Game / Program:
Describe the Program: |

Ease of Play (1-hard to 10-easy):

What are two things you like:

What are two things you would change:

What are two programming blocks (tiles) you think they used to create this program:

Circle your favorite of the three above.

SCRATCH COMMANDS CROSSWORD

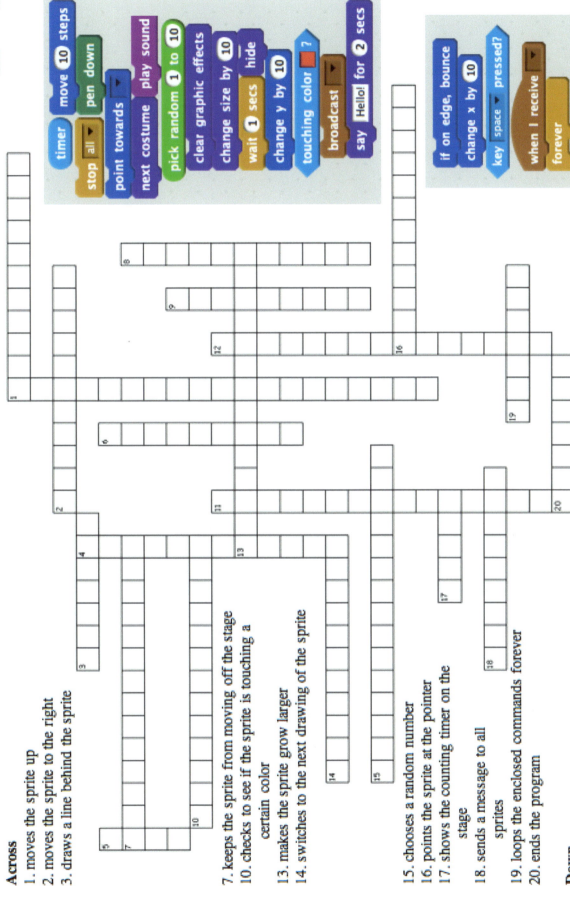

Across

1. moves the sprite up
2. moves the sprite to the right
3. draws a line behind the sprite

7. keeps the sprite from moving off the stage
10. checks to see if the sprite is touching a certain color
13. makes the sprite grow larger
14. switches to the next drawing of the sprite

15. chooses a random number
16. points the sprite at the pointer
17. shows the counting timer on the stage
18. sends a message to all sprites
19. loops the enclosed commands forever
20. ends the program

9. plays a sound
11. shows the sprite saying hello
12. checks to see if the space key is pressed

Down

1. sets all graphics effects to 0
4. waits until a broadcast happens
5. hides the sprite
6. pauses the program for 1 second
8. moves the sprite forward

(Use the code blocks above to fill in the crossword.)

Appendices

Appendix A – The Coordinate System in Scratch

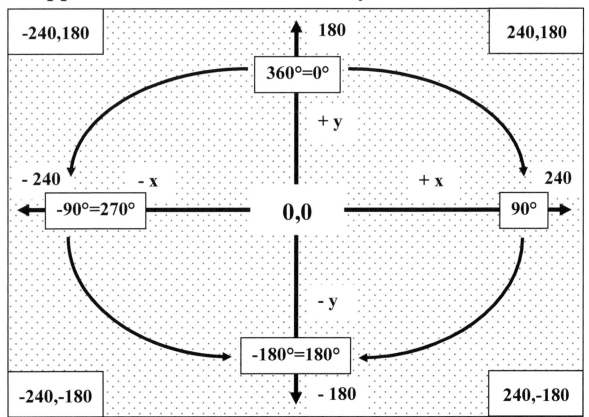

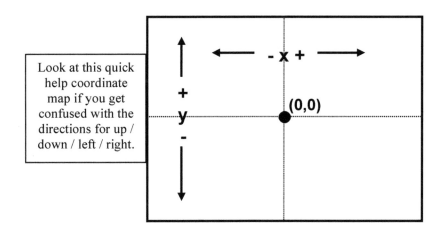

Look at this quick help coordinate map if you get confused with the directions for up / down / left / right.

Appendix B – Using the Paint Editor

(This is a composite image showing several view options at once that will normally only show up one at a time.)

If you make a mistake, the **undo button** is wonderful!

You can **import any sprite** into other sprites, to add a hat, for example, to the cat.

costume1

Clear | Import

Drag the top circle to **rotate** an object.

Many sprite collision problems can be fixed by **resetting the center** of the costume.

Drag the corner boxes to **resize** an object.

Objects drawn in Vector Mode can have their **shapes (points) modified**.

Holding the "SHIFT" key while drawing will make a rectangle a **square** and an oval a **circle**.

Objects drawn in Vector Mode can be moved through **layers**, forwards or backwards.

You can highlight a part of your image to **delete** or hold down the "SHIFT" key and delete everything else.

To **drop out a solid color** background, paint in "nothingness".

The **eyedropper** lets you "suck up" (or select) a color you already have on your canvas.

You can create **interesting blends** by swapping the front and back colors.

The **default** for sprites is zoomed in 200%.

200%

Bitmap Mode

Convert to vector

Line thickness can be controlled with this slider.

You can switch over to the **"rainbow" color picker** if you can't find the exact color you want.

Bitmap Mode is like painting on a single canvas – whatever you add covers up anything under it. You can select an area to modify (move, color, copy), but not the individual objects.

Vector Mode is like painting on multiple canvases that can overlap each other. Shapes created in Vector Mode can be moved as one object, through layers backwards and forwards, and have their points modified.

Appendix C – Music Basics

Modern music is based on scales, a set of 8 notes. The first note is often called the key of the song. The simplest key is C major (sometimes just called C) that starts at middle C (60) and goes up to the next higher C (72). Below is the scale:

C (60) – D (62) – E (64) – F (65) – G (67) – A (69) – B (71) – C (72)

You may notice that the numbers don't change by 2 every time – that is because of the way a major scale is built. The formula for a major scale is 2 whole steps, one ½, 3 whole steps, one ½. Scratch uses 1 step in place of the ½ steps, so the numbering works out to 2-2-1-2-2-2-1 instead of 1-1-½-1-1-1-½.

2 whole steps – 60 to 62 to 64	1 half step – 64 to 65
3 whole steps – 65 to 67 to 69 to 71	1 half step – 71 to 72

The distance from C (60) to C (72) is known as an octave (a complete jump of eight notes in a scale).

The nice thing about the key of C is that on the piano keyboard you don't have to use any of the black keys (sharps/flats), only the white ones, which are the standard ones Scratch makes available to you. You can still select the black piano keys by typing in the number in between the naturals, for instance, using a value of '70' for Bb (which is the same as A#).

Instruments in Scratch	Musical Notes	Percussion
(1) Piano	(72) High C	(1) Snare Drum
(2) Electric Piano	(71) B	(2) Bass Drum
(3) Organ	(69) A	(3) Side Stick
(4) Guitar	(67) G	(4) Crash Cymbal
(5) Electric Guitar	(65) F	(5) Open Hi-Hat
(6) Bass	(64) E	(6) Closed Hi-Hat
(7) Pizzicato	(62) D	(7) Tambourine
(8) Cello	(60) Middle C	(8) Hand Clap
(9) Trombone	(59) B	(9) Claves
(10) Clarinet	(57) A	(10) Wood Block
(11) Saxophone	(55) G	(11) Cowbell
(12) Flute	(53) F	(12) Triangle
(13) Wooden Flute	(52) E	(13) Bongo
(14) Bassoon	(50) D	(14) Conga
(15) Choir	(48) Low C	(15) Cabasa
(16) Vibraphone		(16) Guiro
(17) Music Box		(17) Vibraslap
(18) Steel Drum		(18) Open Cuica
(19) Marimba		
(20) Synth Lead		
(21) Synth Pad		

While this version of Scratch contains fewer instrument and percussion choices than the previous version, all of the ones available seem work work all the time!

Appendix D – Programming Code Help Sheet

when 🚩 clicked
forever
- ▶ **climbing and falling**
- if ⟨ touching Sprite2 ? ⟩ then
  - if ⟨ key up arrow pressed? ⟩ then
    - next costume
    - change y by (3)
  - else
    - change y by (-3)

▶ **slower movement**

when up arrow key pressed
- change y by (10)

when down arrow key pressed
- change y by (-10)

when right arrow key pressed
- change x by (10)

when left arrow key pressed
- change x by (-10)

▶ **smoother movement**

forever
- if ⟨ key up arrow pressed? ⟩ then
  - change y by (10)
- if ⟨ key down arrow pressed? ⟩ then
  - change y by (-10)
- if ⟨ key right arrow pressed? ⟩ then
  - change x by (10)
- if ⟨ key left arrow pressed? ⟩ then
  - change x by (-10)

▶ **shooting a missile**

when space key pressed
- go to Sprite2
- point in direction (direction of Sprite2)
- repeat until ⟨ touching edge ? ⟩
  - move (10) steps
  - if ⟨ touching Sprite3 ? ⟩ then
    - wait (0.02) secs
    - hide
- hide

▶ **jumping**

when space key pressed
- repeat (10)
  - change y by (10)
- repeat (10)
  - change y by (-10)

▶ **highlight an object**

when this sprite clicked
- repeat (50)
  - change color effect by (25)
- clear graphic effects

▶ **scrolling backdrop**

when 🚩 clicked
- set y to (0)
- forever
  - set x to (scrollx + (470) * (1))

when 🚩 clicked
- set scrollx to (0)
- forever
  - if ⟨ key right arrow pressed? ⟩ then
    - change scrollx by (-10)
  - if ⟨ key left arrow pressed? ⟩ then
    - change scrollx by (10)

(scrollx + (10))
((470) * (1))

▶ **bouncing off**

when 🚩 clicked
- forever
  - if ⟨ touching Sprite3 ? ⟩ then
    - point in direction (direction * (180))

Appendix E – Going Further with Scratch-style Programming (Code.org and Snap!)

Code.org is an online campaign to increase the number of students learning to program. Their motto is "Every student in every school should have the opportunity to learn computer science." The online environment uses Scratch-like tile blocks for programming. The website also has very well developed teacher materials, including celebrity videos and the "Hour of Code" project. It has received a great deal of support both from within the field of computer programming (Bill Gates/Microsoft, Martc Zuckerberg/Facebook, Jack Dorsey/ Twitter, Drew Houston/Dropbox) and from outside of it (Chris Bosch/athlete, will.i.am/musician). The website walks students through basic programming concepts, from beginning to more advanced, using popular games, like Angry Birds, Plants vs Zombies., and Flappy Bird. More information can be found at http://en.wikipedia.org/wiki/Code.org and the website is http://code.org/.

Snap! (formerly Build Your Own Blocks) is an extension to Scratch developed by Jens Mönig and Brian Harvey from the University of Cailfornia, Berkeley. It has some of the same additions over Scratch 1.4 that Scratch 2.0 does (such as allowing the user to create their own, customized programming blocks (thus the acronym) and implementing cloning). It also has some advanced concepts that Scratch 2.0 does not have (such as recursion – allowing a command block to 'call' itself). It is very well designed (with a well written manual in Pdf form) and continues to be updated. A more comprehensive description can be found at http://wiki.scratch.mit.edu/wiki/Snap. It is available to run online at http://snap.berkeley.edu. (Saved Snap! projects have a .ypr suffix.)

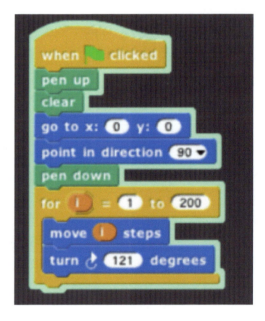